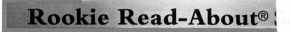

It's a Fruit, It's a Vegetable, It's a Pumpkin

By Allan Fowler

Consultants

Robert L. Hillerich, Professor Emeritus,
Bowling Green State University, Bowling Green, Ohio;
Consultant, Pinellas County Schools, Florida

Lynne Kepler, Educational Consultant

Fay Robinson, Child Development Specialist

CHILDRENS PRESS®
CHICAGO

Design by Herman Adler Design Group
Photo Research by Feldman & Associates, Inc.

Library of Congress Cataloging-in-Publication Data

Fowler, Allan.
    It's a fruit, it's a vegetable, it's a pumpkin / by Allan Fowler.
      p. cm. – (Rookie read-about science)
    ISBN 0-516-46039-0
    1. Pumpkin—Juvenile literature. [1. Pumpkin.] I. Title.
  II. Series.
SB347.F68   1995
641.3'562–dc20   95-5565
                                           CIP
                                           AC

17 18 19 20 21 R 11 10 09 08 07   **08**

What's the biggest
fruit or vegetable
you can think of?

A watermelon may be hard
to lift. But pumpkins grow
even bigger. A pumpkin could
weigh as much as 800 pounds!

Farmers show off their biggest pumpkins at county fairs or state fairs.

Pumpkins grow on vines.
A vine is a plant that
doesn't stand up by itself.

Some vines cling to walls
or trees or posts.

The vines that bear large fruits or vegetables, like pumpkins, grow along the ground.

Melons and cucumbers, zucchini and gourds also grow on vines.

11

Is a pumpkin a fruit or a vegetable? Botanists — scientists who study plants — tell us that a pumpkin is a fruit.

You might think of it
as fruit when you eat
pumpkin pie.

But pumpkin is also served
as a vegetable, or is made
into soup.

In fact, a pumpkin is really
a kind of squash. And
most people call squash
a vegetable.

Among the first people
to raise pumpkins were
Native Americans.

Pumpkins were eaten at
the first Thanksgiving feast
by the Pilgrims in 1621.

Today, pumpkin pie is a favorite dessert, especially with Thanksgiving dinner.

20

There's one time of year
when you see pumpkins
everywhere — Halloween.

Halloween pumpkins
have faces, and are
called jack-o'-lanterns.

You see grinning jack-o'-lanterns in windows if you go trick-or-treating.

You see them at Halloween parties, along with goblins and skeletons, bats and black cats.

To make a jack-o'-lantern,
draw eyes, a nose, and a
mouth on a pumpkin shell
for a grown-up to cut out.

Then scoop out the
pumpkin until it is hollow.

People used to put lighted candles inside jack-o'-lanterns. But it's not a good idea to do that, because a candle can start a fire. A flashlight is much safer.

If a pumpkin is too small to be carved, you can still make a jack-o'-lantern out of it.

Just paint a spooky face on the pumpkin. Spooky — but in a funny way.

You wouldn't want to scare your friends and family.

Or would you?

Words You Know

jack-o-lanterns

pumpkin pie

vines

pumpkin

watermelon

squash

cucumber

Index

About the Author

Allan Fowler is a free-lance writer with a background in advertising. Born in New York, he lives in Chicago now and enjoys traveling.

Photo Credits

©Reinhard Brucker – Hauberg Indian Museum, 17

Chip and Rosa Maria de la Cueva Peterson – 16

PhotoEdit – ©Leslye Borden, 11, 31 (bottom right); ©David Young-Wolff, 13; ©Phil Bordern, 14; ©Myrleen Ferguson, 24

Photri – 18; ©Robert J. Bennett, 4, 31 (top right)

Tom Stack & Associates – ©Inga Spence, Cover

SuperStock International, Inc. – 25; ©Frank Wood, 23, 30 (top left); ©Richard Heinzen, 26

Unicorn Stock Photos – ©Alice M. Prescott, 5; ©Jean Higgins, 7, 30 (bottom); ©Chromosohm/Sohm, 12; ©Martha McBride, 19; 30 (top right); ©Martin R. Jones, 20; ©Ted Rose, 27; ©Denny Bailly, 28

Valan – ©V. Whelan, 8, 31 (top left); ©Kennon Cooke, 15, 31 (bottom left)

COVER: Pumpkins on the vine